THERE ARE LOST FILMS OF US

POEMS BY NICHOLAS GRENN

Contents

FOR YOU.

There Is A Gentle Breeze Behind Us

We're in a field of cherry blossoms,
you and I.
I'm breathing, you know,
you can feel it.

Wind makes gentle petal snow,
my lungs pop open.
Sometimes it isn't so easy
in dark streets,
when I am showered
in what seems like home.
I thought rain
might change me.

Yes, I live in a 5th floor apartment
in an alley where chilling neon
lights blister at window level,
painting pictures
through heavy precipitation,
heavy like a thousand trees
that watch as I lay breathing
beside you.

You're close,
almost like I don't need to speak.
I do, though.

I shoot "I'm sorry"
and "I love you" through a pen;
I know it's next to nothing,
and I know it could be tomorrow
you stop listening, or I stop talking,
but if only I could take you to the forest,
to smell sweet things and sit
in grass blankets and
cherry blossom blizzards,
we would know.
We would breathe in perfect time.

The Moon Didn't Fall, You Just Think It Did

She told me I was looking for liberation,
That I was stuck in all of the wrong places.
I looked for release
In her brown hair, hazel eyes,
Searched for escape
Entwined in her long legs and her small hands.
I listened for her to take
Me back to her
Place with breath loosened sweetly,
footsteps on the pavement of my driveway
Like lips dancing around my neck.
There is liberation in the trees;
Release is in this air that we breathe.
There are one-way tickets
To New York, Seattle, Los Angeles,
Buried beneath this music we hold so close.
There is life in this grass and these roots
Despite our obsession with fire.
There is a storybook ending
In spray paint graffiti
On a train that passes on chipping tracks
While you drive home
From coffee with a woman you love,
And on subway walls and cars,
On their floors and their ceilings, their seats,
Their windows, their passengers,
Underground, beneath a city alive
And painted with people crossing streets
Who only walk when white light says so.
They know exactly where they're headed.

Twenty-Five Minute Drive

I owe my life to a shirt
cobalt, pressed against hums of an engine

my body is thrown to confident wind
and headlights, shined in my windows

I belong to what played on a radio
while automobiles passed beside me

I am a product of advice
that festered like bleach, in my mind and mouth

and those few, still with me or not
who guided me along a jaded path

all these things became a sole moment
outside of myself, to take me outside of

a place I thought was home.

I'm Not Changing, You're Changing

It's been some time
since I've felt.

I don't know when it started
taking me this long to write
about porcelain toilets, spotted mirrors

where you see something that's like you
but not exactly you

because *you* is really just your soul,
the piece of it you left
with your love so you wouldn't lose it

traveling to the moon
but never back. I try to change

for something that looks like you,
that's like you
but not exactly you,

and I'll change everything, piece by piece,
for a chance to float in a pink petal galaxy.

Letters from the Hospital

There's menacing laughter in eerie pines
zipped up in fog, climbing branches
for the best view of the forest dwellers.

I know you don't want to hear from me right now
but I thought you should know
I'm in a place so quiet
I can hear you frantically scribbling
my name from your side of the spectrum.

I'm typing everything
I can remember from my dictionary,
the one I keep in my desk drawer
next to my favorite picture of you.
You know the one I'm talking about,
the one you tried to burn
with enough gasoline to ignite
my words as I write them.
I'm teaching you
a lesson: *my pictures don't burn*
like the others.

While you're busy
dismantling moons,
writing fictional notes on your walls,
I'm trying to make us immortal.

I just want the world to fall in love with me

Seattle

Atop The Needle pointed to the heavens
I sit
clothes soaked
pockets filled

with phone and sopping plane tickets.
Rain rips at my skin.
Between my perch and the ground

air creates a bridge
waiting to be crossed,
tempting me.

I stand
unaware of beyond,
place of solace,
or Hell?

Bliss is absence of identity,
tainted identity,
intrigue may be curiosity of destination.

I'm looking for the top floor
when I'm jolted to a halt pressed against strangers;
this Needle is a broken elevator.

It's Alright If You Want To Leave

We're in a concrete jungle;
    It breathes, inhales
    Dust; people
        Walk on twisted, blistering
Sidewalks that pump
    Stone into your bloodstream.

Traffic
Signals flip
    Around bronze, copper,
Supersonic red beams
On bottom,
And there's writing on
        Top
    Of my hands.

We're in a world where
       Women and
       Men
On their last white pill
Glass
       Bullet
Leap from their apartment windows,
           swap stone with sky.

A poor man lives
In alleyways,
           Streetcars.
       He paints murals,
Gardens, flowers,
Genuine jungles,
        And that is okay.

There Are Lost Films Of Us

It's been three years
or months since you've been dead to me;
Not in the "fuck you" sort of way,
it's more like "I don't remember you."
I've been mixing faces
as much as familiar words and old stories.
Last time I saw you, you were crying

into my dashboard. We were in a friend's driveway
or a dimly lit parking lot or driving
from Farmington to Highland
in a typhoon we conjured.

Sometimes I remember you
with brown hair and sometimes with blonde
and I can't remember where we went
or what songs gave us dances that left us lying together,
but I do remember
we all got sick, pale blue.
My own thoughts terrify me now
because I never know which ghost I'll see next.

I smashed a bottle of your perfume in an act of desperation
to remember what it was like to have your teeth in my
back,

I found glass slices and heart stains on my bedsheets.

I Don't Hear Sirens Yet

Oh how privileged I am!
To catch hurricanes in the webs of my hands,
and stroke hell through my fingers;
to wrap myself with serpents and
asphyxiate a young man
is how I like to pass time.

To rest my head on this pillow
is to float in your ocean,
as I struggle to forget home,
where the two of you hold tight
beside a fire, burning
my letters to you.

So I'll sit in my room,
cut out my tongue,
stain my hands,
smear your name
bright red, three times
on each of my pale walls.

Look at me! I cut all my wires!
Now watch me electrify myself
with every ounce left in my splintered bones,
just to try to pull you from your world
into mine -
just to try to tell you that I'm not okay.

run

there are guns in my closet,
just like everybody else.
they exhale audibly
through cracks in my room.

they're neighbors with my shoes
and an old rope ladder
collecting dust.
I beat them

like cymbals with old pencils
and their dust is not snow.
it's infectious, it's contagious,
it's real.

it's in the house in black and white
where we all once lived,
with a busted doorbell,
shattered windows we threw rocks at,

donning a foreclosure sign
from the worst year of your life
and spray paint on its siding that reads
get the fuck out of here

you see it and stamp out concrete
crying, like you set it on fire,
like you're an amateur
pyrotechnician.

none of us are meant for these slums,
but they still sit vacant, overgrown,
a few blocks away.

tick tock, don't die inside

it's raining,
said the stone clock tower.

its hands shot up
at dark clouds
as if praising gods, pleading
for a moment's peace.

gears turn, they drip and sweat
onto passing cars,
cars with wheels rolling down
wet boulevards in steel harmony,
icy headlights split fog and break
you wide open.

look
you don't have a lot of time
said the crying clock tower.

actually
I'd say you've got about
three minutes
until I'm expired and then
you're still sitting outside,
soaked, but together.

DON'T LEAVE ME HERE ALONE

Syringe

I'm sorry
    I'm sorry.
I didn't mean it,

you know I didn't mean it like *that.*

clocks breathe as I await
    my next dose of morphine,
    my last?

what is the price
paid for this insanity on tap?

  just please say those words
  please!

    I need this, I need
    just one more. If you cared
    at all, just one more

chance
to be "happy"

I see written letters
smoke
      and
            shiny black fingernails
            running through *my* hair.

generator hums cut
hot air at 1 in the morning

      gasoline burns in an engine
      as tears fall and I choke
      out once more

         I didn't mean it

when they know *I fucking did.*

We're Sinners, and Confessions Won't Save Us

I dream this kind of warfare most nights,
where paper shrapnel imprinted with the
letters of your name
is set loose, ablaze with kerosene and black ink.
It's just words on a page, but this Times New Roman
and the crisp corners of a white envelope cut
deeper than a certain, familiar blade.

This is the one where you and I sit
untouched in a parked car, in some backlot
where dimly lit street lamps beckon
bad, and then worse decisions.
This is the part where I tell you,
and you throw open
the passenger door, crying,
kneeling on split pavement.

Now I slump on this floor;
it's 11:48 p.m. and you're starting to learn from this sleep.
I remember this, too. Now it's your turn
to drive somewhere you shouldn't be
and push borders like I'm pushing floorboards.
This is when we decide we don't love each other anymore.

Medicine

My friends got me thinking about them;
pills, I mean.

A nice little plastic bottle
wrapped up and sealed
with our names printed on them.

Grenn, Nicholas

Like a birthday present,
twice a day.

These pills are slaying me,
and no, I'm not on them,
I don't touch them, I don't
even think about taking them
to be honest with you.

And I *am* being honest with you.
That's something they don't have,
something that hasn't been stripped
from me.

So, in response to your questions, no,
I don't like swallowing .50 caliber bullets,
the same ones picking off my friends
one by one in the forest.

The Smell Of Gasoline

I'm on your road
With a Super 8,
Pockets filled, film and batteries
Splitting the seams of the front side
Of my favorite sweatshirt.
Light electric torches and point
At your face as I capture
Fresh lip gloss drip,
Shimmer, glisten, drop,
Splatter at my feet.

You've found my book,
Buried under clothes in your corner,
Witnessing murder and adultery, obscene things.
You've stained it with perfume and a cherry
Red splotch on the cover.
A metal brand singeing skin,
Like your face burned in my head

As you wrap around something else
And I'm crashing cars,
Burning bridges,
Putting my fist through stop lights
On the street.

I hold the spine in my sliced hands,
Run paper through my fingers, damp,
Not crisp like when I took the thing home
For the first time.
A story I've read, 18 years,
You're the author now.
Scratch your name
On the cover, back, pages.

Put your pen through
My tongue, look how my ink
Spills out like your gloss.

Mojave Desert

Force the undersides
of your shoes into sand,
turning leaflets of your favorite characters,
crazy fiction, into petals from flowers,
food for nature.

I never got my book
back, a piece of everything
I wanted you to learn. I tried
to teach you that storied endings
stay bound within our pages.

You visit every now and then,
usually late at night when I'm not around.
That same crazy fiction
tells me all about it.

> *She came by and saw you,*
> *sands twisting like they were drinking*
> *the soul right out of you.*
> *They were dying of thirst.*
> *So were you. She left you*
> *with another few months to breathe.*
> *Sing while you can.*

Bright crystals cut me open,

and I sung. With my last
drops of red life
I sung scared and nervous, but I sung for you.
A voice unfamiliar poured out,
kissing my ears. It felt like the entire
world came to listen, except for you.
My lungs tore apart like my leaflets,
vocal chords deteriorated beneath an immense pressure.

Still, I wonder if you hear my music, and I wonder
if the rhythm makes you move like it makes me move,
and I wonder if you dance
like in my imagination, and I wonder
if you ever think of me.

Lotus

When I first saw her
she was drinking sweet nectar
in the garden between
the Moon and the Sun.
She wore nature, was nature,
hair so long
it reached
all the way to where I was
standing, carried me,
pulled me in close. That's when
I heard her soft and small breath
for the first time,
a rabbit moving precious and slow
through grass that keeps it almost hidden.

She breathed into my body and kissed my soul.

Her lips on my core
were foreign and strange
and so beautiful. It was an experience
that I think was unlike anything
any other man had ever known.
Only myself and any other beings
in her unearthly realm.

I'll never forget what I felt in the garden.
we were both greeted by the sea
and we smiled together.

The Last Time I Prayed

I was ready to take the time machine back
to your place. That should've been
my first clue. It was warming up
when I saw you run to me in the driveway
and you held me and kissed me
like it was air and you hadn't been breathing.
Your lips were just how I had left them.

We watched art together,
cinema and sculpture and paint,
we took it all in
as one and we became it,
I swear.

You brought me gifts,
I wasn't expecting you so
I gave you something personal instead.

We talked about the moon,
how we share the same
moon every night,
how we would look at it and
it made us feel
like I wasn't far from you, and
you weren't far from me.

For once, we cried together.
You asked me where I'd been,
and I said I was sleeping.
I opened my eyes.

Don't Think I'm Not As Scared As You Are

This house is getting old.
Paint chips, splits, flakes;
foundations become one with dirt.

I'm loading my things
piece by piece into a moving truck
with rusted wheels and ancient headlights.

I wonder if we have working brakes.
She told me not to worry,
"You'll make it there, I'm right beside you."

We drive under streetlights,
neon and white gas.
They're psychic, the lights.

My face freezes and the air
conditioning in our truck
hums in pitch black. I'm guessing

those lights are reading
my mind about now,
they know where I'm going.

They feel wavering vapor
spilling from slumber
beneath flickering beams, frosted traffic signs.

We're precocious. We're terrified.
We're wading in an electric ocean.

We've Been Gone So Long
I Almost Don't Remember Your Voice

I dreamt of you again.
Most of it slipped away,
but I held onto the part where
you were holding me
and that it was the first time
in a long time
that I've felt like myself.

You grabbed my wrists
tight, like you were trying to stop
them from bleeding.

They were never bleeding,
but you wouldn't have ever
let that happen.

Tight,
like we had just found
our old stash
of sugar-coated
methamphetamine.

I burned that box where we kept
our medicine,
and with our pictures,
at the end of last year.

You cried about the drugs,
not about our pictures.

I'm thinking back on it now,
I guess I don't know
if it was really you
or someone who looked just like you.

I'm still sitting
in the cherry blossom fields,
just in case you feel
like coming back for a while.

Willow

You don't quite feel like getting up today.
I think it's the way the sun lights your eyes,
Or it might be the way that it doesn't sometimes.
How did you find your way to this bed?
Figure it out, or don't;
They're waiting for you.
Your life is dictated by numbers on display,
A truth we all face.
I know you're tired, that you don't understand,
But numbers say that it's time to go now.

They know better than you do.

So shake the dust off your jeans;
The waist is too tight now.
Sweat out your weary pores,
Wipe rain from your face,
Kick leaves from your path,
Trudge through snow.
Scrawl your name in it, let them know you were here.
And when that snow starts to soak your knees,
Take a sip from your cardboard cup,
Rub your hands with warm breath.

Carry on.

Pull that wrench out from your side.
Trembling, but breathing,
Scream to those who choose to listen:
"I am not a medic!"
Throw your sole on the brakes;
This road you're on
Leads not to redemption, or a hospital,
Or the house of that girl you thought you loved,
But to a grave
Beneath a slouching willow, coated with ice,

Where your mother will weep and weep and weep.

Beached

I shattered a porcelain mug
on the floor of a diner. I swear
it was an accident,
the waitresses don't look
like they believe that.

I was with an older gentleman.
He was from the future,
wearing a torn up blue sweatshirt
like he found it on the shore,
under a palm tree that listens
to the gentle music this man plays.

He told me tales of adventure,
of living in jungles, surviving
with the rain (he lived for three years
on rainwater alone, he told me).
They can't hear all the noise out there, he said.

He described different prostitutes
that he had come to know
in the big city. One, by the name
of Serenity, or at least
that's what she called herself,
was addicted to heavy narcotics.

They had been friends, not in business,
for roughly half a year, fall and winter,
until he went to her apartment
in the harsher part of the neighborhood.
It was his birthday. He found first
her door open, and then
after stepping inside, her body,
sat up on the floor against a suede couch.
Blood dripped from her nose, a small
amount, about the size of a fingertip.

He didn't say goodbye,
nor did she.

It was at this point
in our strange conversation that his eyes
started to drip. He knew he couldn't stay,
and apologized for leaving so soon.
His eyes were deep. He had much more to tell me.

reasons to stay alive and transparent

you can't see it, but you feel it
pressing under
your rib cage
when you hold me
tight enough.

      truthfully, I don't even load it.
      I couldn't,
      I've never owned bullets.
      just sort of like to
           aim
      at things.

I want everyone
to know that I love you all,
and you wonder
how much, and I say so much
that when it's raining and
you push me back
to back with the brick wall
outside my apartment building every
now and then
and dare me
to pull my trigger, I
      aim, click
      nothing.

it's still raining.
we're all still standing.

I Won't Die In San Francisco

I sat on the bridge
against one of its big tall pillars,
wished you were on another one.

An older woman walked by me.
She was around the age
of seventy or so.

She had gray hair, but I could tell that it used to be brown,
like mine.
Strolled up, looked me up and down, like she had a
dictionary
of all her experiences of all the existential issues I could be
having,
and she was looking me up in her ancient book.

What are you doing here alone?

I've just had my heart broken,
and to be quite honest I felt like sitting up here
and staring into the water at the bottom of the bridge,
all that way down. I've been thinking about how many people
have probably jumped from this very spot.
It makes me sad, I'm supposed to be feeling sad right now.
I've just had my heart broken,
I think this is what I'm supposed to be doing right now.

Well, you're going to need this.

      (she threw me an oxygen mask. we shared glances
of affirmation and she went.)

In Bad Neighborhoods

Your dress is falling off,
melting, bleeding
onto broken pavement.

There is a faint whistle
from pipe veins
strung along
brick fortress walls
on either side of you.

A scarred door on the left
is open, about an inch.
Blue light spills out
onto one of your shoulders,
and half of your face.
You're shaking.

All I can do
is sit beside you
in your melting dress.
You press your hand into mine.

It's not that
we have nothing to say
or that we don't want to speak,
it's that we can't,
like the air is the only thing
holding us together,
and if we breathe
a single syllable
we'll collapse
right then and there in the alley.
But I think if you could,
you'd ask me
in a petrified whisper,
why we haven't gotten up
and walked
along the well-lighted sidewalks
to take you wherever
your home is.

I'm Not Finished Yet

There is an orange street
lamp warming my side,
             but it isn't quite warm enough
             to replace your head
nestled safely on my chest.
It used to be
that all I could talk about was
       where we were or what we were doing
but my words are your warmth,
           gone
left me beneath this lonesome
soulless orange street lamp.
               I swear it's like I can feel
those tears you left on my neck
in the raindrops bleeding
into my backside.

I don't like being forceful
      but this wrench
      that I plunged into the side of
my heart is still there.
I'm still breathing but like you

I am also still bleeding;

blood stains quick.

I told this lamp my secret
and I told it to give you my message
but it isn't listening, unsurprisingly,

so

if you're reading this,
there's one thing that I want
to let you know, and it's that
I'm scared,
but I still feel
you in the air.

Block

I turn to elixir,
my remedy for heart and headache;
this time it's tasteless,
my mind remains numb.
a glance into my inventory reveals tools
I used to combat depression,
broken.

floor and sky now my only company,
my doctors of yesterday,
my friends,
have morphed.
they are fog
hovering over a wrecked vehicle
and its leaking driver.

I sit in front of blank canvas,
splotches of red, yellow,
blue, and green,
wait on a palette.
pigments drip onto the floor,
colliding until the hue shifts undesirably.
I need new paint.

Massacre Pond

drowning in cool violet shades,
I can feel your body through them.
we are connected
through a sea of indigo and fuchsia.

you send scarlet kisses
on ocean waves,
I send back prayers.

there are an infinite number
of possible higher powers
watching us float,
I put my faith in you.

I don't know if you'll resurrect
my soul, I don't think
the others will.

dear spirit,
I sense you
swimming with me. close,
not enough. dear spirit,

the water is imbued with your electricity.
are you reviving me, or ending me?
can you show me an afterlife?

you still haven't told me where we're headed

       I really just like talking,
but I guess that's lethal
like pretty girls
that smell like fruit and ask how
my day was
or how I'm feeling
       I'm falling in love with you
is what I would've said
had I not been pulling threads
out of fresh toxic sheets on my bed
       I would've spilled onto the ground,
a cloudy puddle you splashed in
as a kid, laughing,
smiling,
because there's nothing scarier
than yelling in theaters,
at empty aluminum chairs,
electric constellations falling apart
twenty feet from my head
trying to drown out ticking
from a working clock that's faster
than mine is
       likewise, soft hands wrapped
around my own are
the most weakening things I know of

there's another car in the driveway
bathing in my moonlight

I'm stretched on the roof of my home

wandering headlights peer into me
just so long as I stay up here,
whispering secrets with the oak trees
and their autumn stained leaves

trees don't run like cars do

Highland Recreation Area

At 1:38 a.m. I watched
a Ford Focus drill into
pine trees on the oncoming side
of the road. The driver side door
opened, a bloodied
sixteen-year-old
slid out.
He was hammered, he had
my face.
I laid him down
on a bed of needles
and pinecones beside me.
I looked in his car,
it was filled with Versace perfume,
letters that looked like maps.
I read them,
some were about a blonde girl, others about
dying,
a few about both.

I never called 911.
A woman filling up at the Mobil,
two miles or so away,
called to report a Ford Focus
that passed at about
90 miles per hour. It appeared
to be stolen. Police arrived
and saw me bathing in
blue and red light,
standing over him,
in his pine needles.
My clothes were stained with him.

LUNGS

there was once a phoenix
that died inside your eyes.
clawed at the back of your pupils
until your eyes burst open
with fire, passion. rebirth,

reasons you stopped pulling
into my driveway, tongues in
your pistons just like in your retinas
the first time I ever looked into them.

I heard "death" whispered
by a notebook wearing
dust and my sixteen-year-old blood.
it's wrong, not death,
just the wrong season.
how could I blame it, though?
your heat wave explosion
feels plenty like death
standing a few feet away.

your waves crawl down my throat,
seal my lungs,
put hands in my hair that run
down my cheeks and grasp
my face. they close in
to kiss me, pull away
with just a few molecules between
their lips and mine.

when I say I can still feel
your thumbs on my mouth,
I mean to say that every night
at around 11:13 p.m. I have
no choice but to sit on a couch
beside you and feel
your breath on my neck,
your grip on my bones.

if I could twist my heart
I'd do it in a single beat, but
I have no choice
except to let you go
not once, but every night
since the first time
you left me breathless,
bleeding in the dark.

"It's Not Murder If You Get Away With It"

I could feel holes in my skin,
they only bled slowly.
I don't remember
much else, except being draped
on roots and thinking maybe
I could stop my bleeding
if I stuffed my guts
with some moonlight
and strewn oak leaves.

then I thought

maybe it would be better
if I finished what you started,
grabbed a branch
a few feet away,
drove it clean through
one of the leaks in my chest.
it wouldn't be the worst

way to go out, stars watching,
put to sleep beneath
a plummeting moon.

       I just needed to feel
       your heat drop;

I think that'd be enough
to remember
what you looked like

with your hand on your trigger,

what you looked like
fully loaded.

I wish I could recall
how you described
the weight of your bullets,
your grip on your handle.

I'd rewind to your eyes
as your stare danced down
your barrel and collided
with my own.

I wish I could say for sure
that I stared back across the steel
and told you to make sure
you emptied your clip.

I wonder
how afraid
you must've been
to use only three shots,
then run.

Multi-Dimension

There is an ocean
with teardrop salt
and confetti
creatures of the deep,
ones that match those

in the Pacific. It is
untouched.
Waves that match

waves flowing from me
to you. There is a sunset

with a shade the same
as every first kiss
on black sand
beaches below. Soft as
young hearts who kissed them.

There are colors
man has not seen.
I learned this
on a voyage through eyes
of a being

I do not comprehend.

I haven't seen them
yet, but I'm betting
that when I do,
I'll feel
the same

hands grabbing my face,
soul in my throat
feeling that you send
back to me
on our waves.

"Who Says You Need To Buy A Guitar?"

Two nights ago, there was
a meteor shower that spit
boiling tears as venom,
tears from when I was a child.

It rained on me from beyond
the atmosphere.

Screams on their way down
spilled out of each one
and singed my skin
like broken fireworks.

They sounded like I did;
      the first time I coped with death
I was ten years old.

I strapped broken glass
from Cherry Coke bottle-and-fury concoctions
into tree branch slingshots and tried to beam
their souls out of the sky, back
to flesh and lips
so that they could kiss me like
the meteors did.
Arms that could wrap me up
like carbon
in a way that whispered in my ears,
not to tell me

It's okay to cry

but in a way that whispered,

> We're all red bullets in space.
> When you slingshot back down,
> aim for the river.
> Don't crash alone.

She Was Right, There Was No Way Out

Often, I find myself asking everyday questions,
like what I'll wear for the day, if I'm seeing anyone,
what's stopping me from driving headfirst
into oncoming traffic, or why stars lull me to sleep,
but not quick enough for me to skip the part
where I torture myself with your scars.
That part is my favorite. It's where I lay on my back,
travel through words, the sky, the ocean, and big cities
where you can hide your body in a sheet with two holes.
Say you're a ghost and people treat you like one too.

That part of the night is where I get to stab myself
in my gut like I'm sixteen again, then wonder
if I'm good enough to put my broken pieces into words
like I used to. I didn't know real pain
until I saw you and had to pray every single time
that it wouldn't be the last time. I'll drown myself
in the lake behind my house before I let it dry up.
If you ever find me back there, in the bottom of a crater
wearing seaweed and a fishbone crown,
walk home, it's all over. I'm dead for sure.

CHALLENGER

I have to stop and take a guess
at the number of cameras pointed at me
at this moment.

How many *eyes* are on me?

      I'm starting to freeze.

They're watching
like they know that I'm choking, they know
fuel and sweat
are about to start opening
weak shuttle walls.
I thought I would break out of our atmosphere,
I want to be up close and personal with the stars,
ocean waves always call out to me.

I have to stop and take a guess
at how my name came out
of John Kennedy's mouth,
which of my stories ended
up on all that 8-millimeter film.
I wonder what kind of faces I pressed
onto humanity's plastic.

I hope they didn't find them in the ocean.
I hope I didn't leave them
there.